MOUNTAINS

25 DEVOTIONALS WITH JAKE LUHRS

JAKE LUHRS

HeartSupport, Inc.
PO Box 19461
Austin, TX 78760
info@heartsupport.com
www.heartsupport.com

Graphic Design by Kevin Schrecengost

For John
You really did show up

CONTENTS

I never thought I'd write a book, let alone a devotional. To be honest, I didn't think the day would come when I would share some of my proudest (and not so proud) moments with an audience who might even care to listen.

I know not all of this devotional makes me look like the greatest guy, but in the process of writing it, I realized the goal of this devotional has nothing to do with me. Through the stories told here, the trials, good and bad, my goal is to point people to Christ, or to realize maybe something is lacking in their relationship with Christ. I hope that as you read through these pages you open yourself more to God and see what a deeper relationship with him could become.

I share these sentiments because the one consistent person through my struggles and successes (as you will soon read about) has been my Dad (God).

If you know anything about me you know I don't push "religion." I don't want to promote a religion, and I certainly don't want to hurt anyone with a religion. But I do want people to have the same *relationship* I have with Jesus. I want them to feel loved and understood. When they're scared, I want them to see him as the ultimate source of love, hope, help, strength, and forgiveness. I want you, *dear reader*, to also trust him this way and be able to forgive others and heed his direction in your life or recognize areas that you need to change. I hope that through my transparency you'll see this process is messy, but it's intimate and passionate and nothing on earth compares.

If you're not sure what you think or believe about Christ, then I hope this book encourages you to take a deeper look at who you are. Perhaps even look at why you respond to the world the way you do, and how you've become the person you have. I hope it challenges you to pursue your dreams and love others the way you want to be loved regardless of the color of their skin, who they're in love with, what they believe in, what they've done, or what's been done to them.

I have to give a big thanks to Ben Sledge for editing these stories and devotionals for me. As I wrote them from the heart, a lot of what I wrote came out sounding pretty nasty, messy, confusing, and difficult to understand. I'm thankful that throughout the years of our friendship he's come to understand the way I communicate and my intentions. *Thank-you, friend.* You not only made me sound smart, but did a wonderful job translating my heart onto these pages. I also want to thank his wife, Emily, for her help with the editing process and questions for this devotional. Her heart is like mine, so thank you for all you did to make this devotional a success.

I also want to thank HeartSupport and August Burns Red. Over the years they've seen the highs and lows and have come to my aid or celebrated with me. I don't have words to express my gratitude to Brent, Dustin, JB, Matt, Nate, Ben, Dan, Casey, John and the rest of our teams. But most of my thanks goes directly to these men. They've seen and heard all of me and been a support system in their own way, each supporting my dreams and desires to lead others (and myself) toward healthy spiritual and mental wholeness.

Finally, I want to thank my parents and sister. They are amazing people and featured in some of these stories. While you may think this devotional might tell a story of division in my family, it's truly a story of forgiveness. As my family has gone through a variety of trials—all while doing what they thought was best at the moment—forgiveness stood and love conquered. My family means the world to me, and I wouldn't be the man I am today without their encouragement, love, sacrifice and devotion. They've helped me to become well-rounded, more understanding, and they continue to cheer for me.

I hope this book leads many to their own story of forgiveness. My great hope is love is victorious in the lives of each person who picks up this book.

Oh. I almost forgot to thank my dog, Winston. The little dog that could . . . 'cause he's my son.

If you're just picking up this book and don't know who I am or what HeartSupport does, the contents inside may seem off the beaten path for a devotional. HeartSupport—the nonprofit organization that produced this workbook (and to which all proceeds go)—works directly in the hard rock and metal music industry providing fans the resources they need. The reason why we work inside the music industry is because I'm a vocalist (though some would say I scream for a living) in a twice Grammy-nominated metal band named August Burns Red. God gave me the vision for this ministry when I began hearing from my fans at the merch table after our shows. They would express how much my band's lyrics impacted them and then go on to share about addiction, depression, suicide ideation, hopelessness, despair, anxiety, self-harm, and numerous other mental health issues. So I wanted to do something besides a five-minute pep talk at the merch table each night. I wanted to create a place where people could come exactly as they are—broken or whole—and live connected in community and with their hurts and pains on display. I, too, try to live as authentically as I can with my flaws and shortcomings on display, because I ask the men and women at HeartSupport to do the same. As HeartSupport's influence has grown, more Christians have stepped forward sharing their struggles within the realm of mental health and faith. They feel the overwhelming pressure to appear perfect, and thus act fake for their church leaders and friends. As you'll discover in this devotional, I felt that pressure too. However, that mentality is not the core of what HeartSupport is, nor what Christ calls us to do.

At HeartSupport, we are a raw and authentic community. All of us struggle with sin and darkness in our heart. As of late, story after story has come forth of pastors and church leaders in scandals. I think the pressure is to play pretty, and so they hide the darkness that lurks about until they get caught. If I were to pretty up portions of this devotional for the sake of appearing more "Christian," then I'd be another fraud with a platform, not sharing the dark parts of my heart and sin that God asks me to confess.

So this is a warning to let you know that if you're expecting some rated G, Sunday school version of life, you're in the wrong place. This is about the mountains and dark valleys we face and how God can help us overcome them. In the pages of this book you'll hear curse words, shocking stories, and my shortcomings—many in the past few years.

I don't put these things in here to be relevant or "hip." I tell stories the way they are because that's what happened, *curse words and all*. However, if you're worried about profanity in this devotional and me slighting God, I would ask you consider the following.

The Scriptures are full of obscene language and stories. In the book of Ezekiel alone, the prophet talks about huge penises, female fluid produced at sexual arousal, and large quantities of semen being "poured out" on Israel. Ezekiel then reminds

Israel that they are God's wayward whore (see Ezekiel 16:26, 36, 37; 23:20–21). Much of what we see in our translations is a sanitizing of the language, and many clergy avoid the root words. The Apostle Paul also uses the vulgar word for excrement when he states, "I have suffered the loss of all things and count them as rubbish" (see Phil. 3:8, ESV). Translators once again, cleaned up the language and chose the word *rubbish*. Additionally, Christians invent curse words that aren't curse words (dang, shoot, darn, son of a bee sting, what the flip) that make us sound even more absurd to an unbelieving world. Jesus reminds us that if we mean it in our hearts, we said it no matter how much we cleaned it up.

All this to say, sometimes to convey the emotion and reality of the situation, it's appropriate to tell the events as they happened instead of lying about them to make myself look better. The biggest charge against Christians is that we're hypocrites. Many Christians have no problem watching R-rated movies or reading books where there's plenty of cursing, so I trust that you will understand my choice to offer a raw look at life here. Because I don't want to come under fire before this devotional even begins I felt the need to explain. It's not littered with "bad" words, but you will encounter a few. My prayer is that you'll see a picture of what happens when God takes darkness and brings it into light when you let the Holy Spirit do his work in you.

I'm hoping that happens for you in these pages.

God Bless,

Jake Luhrs

"If I could speak all the languages of earth and of angels, but didn't love others, I would only be a noisy gong or a clanging cymbal. If I had the gift of prophecy, and if I understood all of God's secret plans and possessed all knowledge, and if I had such faith that I could move mountains, but didn't love others, I would be nothing. If I gave everything I have to the poor and even sacrificed my body, I could boast about it, but if I didn't love others, I would have gained nothing."

—1 CORINTHIANS 13:1-3

If you're like me you've gotten in some fierce debates before. If you're a Christian, then the chances of you getting into a dumb debate over theology are even higher. They can be silly things like "Was the Earth created in six days or six billion years?" or "Well, I think this is what God *really* asks of us." In each instance, the words and the way I use the Bible wasn't coming from a place of love. I had a tendency to use Christ to back up my personal agenda or get what I wanted. Whether that was to look intelligent, appear to know what I was talking about, or feel I was a better person, none of it came from a place of love.

For years I've resented the Church. When you're the guy who screams on stage for a living and covered in tattoos, you can get a lot of looks. I always felt judged simply walking through a church door combined with the fact no one ever seemed to struggle either. Instead, it was all smiles and "praise the Lord." I got over my hang-up, but those feelings led to one of those argumentative debates when I was visiting a church in Seattle. The argument started when one of the men I was talking with after service took a very strong stance about predestination (the belief that God chooses you to be saved and you have no choice in the matter) and the elect (the belief that Christ only died for those he planned to save, not the rest of the world).

So what happened?

Man, *we went at it.* We were like two dogs in a fight, neither backing down. Looking back, the whole situation was pathetic and embarrassing. But it's a great example of me throwing my beliefs—and the Bible—around to prove others wrong. In effect, I was just as judgmental as the people I felt were judging me. There was no love in our conversation, and in that moment, I realized I was nothing more than a "noisy gong." Nothing in my words or actions showed Christ's love or his mercy for others. I was thrashing another human being's morals, values, and lifestyle to prove I was better. *Where's the love in that?*

When I think of my relationship with God, the first thing that comes to mind is that He loves me. God genuinely loves me and wants to be part of my life. He desires and enjoys me spending time with him and vice versa. I also dwell on His grace and mercy. Every morning I think about how He's given me forgiveness I don't deserve and covers my poor decisions in grace. He's done so much to ease my soul, mind, and body from suffering as well. Just as God has shown me tremendous mercy and love, he has imparted to me the ability to show mercy and love

In 1 Corinthians 13:1-3 Paul has a conversation with the Corinthian church to explain just how important love is. The church had been using their spiritual gifts in a destructive manner that left people alienated. *Sound familiar?* Instead, he encouraged them to use their gifts in love and for the building up of one another, *not as noisy gongs.*

Many people can do the "Christian" thing. We can talk to people about Scripture, we can share the good news, and we can tithe to our church or donate to a cause. We can even read our Bibles and proclaim to others how much we love Jesus. But if these things don't flow out of love, then what are we doing? *And why are we doing it?*

When we read the Bible, if we aren't doing it out of a place of love, then why are we reading it? Is it so we can discover some life hack to feel better? If we tell someone how much Jesus has done in our lives without the root of our message or testimony coming from a place of love, then why are we sharing it? For our own benefit? If we share the gospel or talk about scripture with others and it isn't rooted in love, then what good is it?

Far too often, Christians are seen as hypocrites who use Scripture to hurt, shame, and guilt others. But Paul reminds us to build up others in love, and Jesus reminds us we'll be known for our love. When we condemn others with our words and actions, Christ's sacrifice on the cross and what he's accomplished to free us from the burden of condemnation becomes inept.

We must first love. Then through our personal relationship with God, he can show us how to love people in the moment.

The world needs to know about the loving, gracious, merciful, redeeming, forgiving, and living God. The depth of His love shows through his willingness to have His own son die for us while we were still enemies with God (see Romans 5:8). But how is that love shown and communicated? Through you, through me, and through those who have an intimate relationship with God in Christ.

The call is clear. We must become loving, supportive, encouraging, generous, uplifting, sensitive to others' hurt and pain, and non-judgmental. Let us challenge ourselves to make love more actionable than condemnation, and, please, don't do what I did and use the Bible to demean or belittle someone. Let's ditch the noisy gong. Instead let's be known for our love since Christ first loved us.

1. Where do you need to change or repent in areas where you've used your faith in destructive manners?

2. Who can you encourage today or build up in love?

And we know that God causes everything to work together for the good of those who love God and are called according to His purpose for them.

—ROMANS 8:28

There's a story I don't usually speak about publicly due to how much it affected my life. The experience crippled me, but I feel the need to share it here.

In 2015 my wife and I divorced, and the fallout was devastating. I spiraled into a deep, dark depression. I woke up every day empty and hollow. This may shock you to hear from a "Christian," but I would wake up at three in the afternoon just so I could start drinking again. I received all kinds of hate messages:

"You're not a real Christian."

"What about 'til death do us part'?"

"Welp, that didn't last long."

These messages coupled with my drinking was a perfect storm.

I understand it isn't easy being a married and touring musician, but our problems went beyond that. It's difficult being in the spotlight when your world falls apart, so I isolated and remained hopeless. Thoughts ran through my head: *Who am I now? I'll never have a family. No one will ever love me again. No one wants the **divorced** guy. I'm a failure.* It was a constant refrain playing again and again. To shoot you straight, I also stepped out of my role at HeartSupport because I knew I wasn't fit to lead it. Ben Sledge and Nate Hilpert ended up running the organization for two years before I found healing. Just when I felt I'd lost everything, one evening, sitting on my porch talking to God, the truth hit me. While praying to God I heard a voice in my head say:

> *You're no longer the leader of a nonprofit ministry. You're not on tour for the next four months, so you aren't the singer of August Burns Red. You're no longer a husband to a wife. These are all things you've looked to for security and relied upon for your identity. But you can't hide yourself in these any longer. Come with me and let's find you—who you really are. Let's see who Jake Luhrs truly is. Stop searching for validity in your works on earth. I want you to feel validated in knowing you are my son.*

A few months later my band, August Burns Red, had a headliner in the United States. My ex-wife and I agreed to make public an Instagram post about our divorce, so people knew about the divorce once I was back on the road. But while on the tour, God took my brokenness and used it for good.

One evening after a show while greeting fans, a young man

almost broke into tears and asked if we could talk. We stepped away from the crowd to a deserted area near a payphone. "Jake, I know you just went through a divorce. Well, my wife and I," he confided. "Well, it looks like we're headed the same direction. Right now we're separated, and I just need advice."

It's hard enough to go through a divorce but the stigma attached to being divorced in the Church can be crushing. No one stands at the altar thinking their marriage will fail. No one plans for this to happen. And here was this guy whose pain I understood. Someone who needed an ear and advice. He needed to hear he wasn't alone, so I shared from my heart. I shared ways in which he could fight for his marriage. Ways in which he could establish boundaries and build trust and lessons from my mistakes. Then I prayed for him.

Divorce is never easy. Eventually, God removed the shame I felt and replaced it with love and acceptance. I began to see the good and beautiful amidst my failure and learned to forgive myself. I'm still in the process of finding my worth not in what I do, but in what Christ has done for me. However, that moment by the payphone was the moment God began to change me for the better. I got to experience firsthand how my platform with August Burns Red and my struggles could be used for good. I survived the drought and darkness and God made what once looked unredeemable into something that could help others. My divorce, depression, and drinking now were a catalyst to point people to God's unconditional love.

The apostle Paul wrote a letter to church in Rome in which he says that God causes "everything to work together for the good of those who love God" (Romans 8:28). At first glance, that's a big pill to swallow. How on earth could suffering and hardship be good? With so many issues and injustices in the world, how's that even possible? For the man or woman caught on the dwarf planet of depression or who have been through divorce, it's hard to see anything as "good."

But I'm always reminded of my story and how God used evil for good.

Romans 8:28 is a verse I never wanted to hear when I was going through my divorce, but now it's a balm to my soul. Now it allows me to face the future with confidence because God doesn't take our angst or suffering lightly. He doesn't dismiss your crippling times of depression or fear. He cares about the mountains you face and the trials you're in. If he didn't, *then nothing good would ever come out of our pain.*

In every problem—big or small—God is the answer. When you reach the end of the tunnel, he's the one standing there. Just maybe God is using all our broken stories for his good, and if we'll let him, those stories can point others to his unconditional love.

The question is, will you let him?

1. What's a mountain in your life currently? Are you struggling in a relationship? Are you unable to find work? Can you not shake a particular sin? Where are you hurting and where don't you trust God for it to turn out well? Lay it all out. He's big enough to handle it.

2. Look back at one of the hardest things that's happened in your life. Did you become stronger because of it? In retrospect, do you see now how God worked during the hard times when you weren't able to see him in the midst of the moment?

No one can serve two masters. For you will hate one and love the other; you will be devoted to one and despise the other. You cannot serve God and be enslaved to money.
—MATTHEW 6:24

I can vividly remember the day I gave up and dove headfirst into my sin. The day I signed the papers after a traumatic divorce was the day I spiraled. "Why'd you let this happen, God?" I asked over and over. My anger at God combined with the guilt and shame I felt, drove me to the edge.

When people go through traumatic events, they often turn to something to help them cope: social media, drugs, self-harm, relationships, or, in my case, alcohol. Booze became my coping mechanism. I had always drank sparingly (in moderation), but in the midst of my valley of darkness, I gave in to the monster rampaging in my soul. Every night I'd wander over to a bar and drown my feelings till I could barely stand and my eyes were bleary. There were four bars within walking distance, so each night I'd find myself at a new one, drowning my sorrows and isolated from the people who cared about me. Each night I'd stumble home, talk drunkenly to God, cry, and pass out.

One evening I drank so much a friend had to come pick me up. In my inebriated state I cursed God. I was so angry because of the events I'd been through that I punched my friend's dashboard and then rolled down the window and screamed at God: "Let's go! You and me, you fucking cunt!" Some of you are appalled that I could call my Savior such a horrible word, let alone that I included it in a devotional. As I said in the introduction, however, real life is messy. I'm not proud I said it, but keep reading because I *need* you to see God's response.

When we pulled into my friend's driveway, I stumbled out of the car and continued to scream at the sky, demanding that God "come down and fight me." I told him I was tired of being a role model, tired of fitting in with Christian culture, that I was over the pain, and that the weight was too much. As I punched the ground it rained. Then it poured. Sitting there on my hands and knees crying, I had a vision of God crying too. His heart broke for me, and he didn't want to fight me. He wanted to love me.

That brief vision didn't stop me from serving my other god, it only provided a brief glimmer of hope. I still wanted to be numb. I'd tried multiple counselors, read books, and went through programs before my divorce. I was at the end. *I planned to tap out.* I wasn't strong to endure.

A couple weeks after my breakdown and hitting my friend's dashboard, I called my dad. I had to hear it from him. "What's the meaning of life?" I asked. "Why are we here?"

I'd wrestled through the question before: *To live your life well,* I thought. *Make the world a better place, right? Then you die and another generation does the same thing. And then they die. Is that it?* It was as if I were climbing a never-ending mountain. What's the point?

"Jake," my father began. "I don't have an answer other than that I believe we're supposed to make a small section of this world better than how we found it." I appreciated his effort, but it wasn't good enough for me. I ended up going off on a rant letting him know I was "done trying to climb that mountain." I was ready to admit defeat.

"You're a good man," he continued. "One of the best I know. You've accomplished so much in your life, but if you don't quit drinking, even those questions will be meaningless. It will end and you'll have nothing."

That was the hard truth I needed to hear. It opened my eyes to the fact that I was worshipping another god besides the one I'd given my heart to. That evening I went home and poured every drop of booze down the drain. I didn't want my mind and thoughts controlled by another "master." I wanted Christ to be master and his love to permeate my life. I was tired of running and numbing out. For the next six months every day I made a decision toward sobriety to ensure I didn't take a single sip of alcohol.

In our lives, we all worship something. It can be a relationship, success, fame, money, work, sports, or even our identity. We take sips off these gods, become intoxicated by them, and serve them—often unknowingly. What we serve becomes our master, and when I served alcohol, it became my master. Whatever is utmost in our lives, whatever we say, "if I were to lose this, then life would be over" is what we worship.

Whatever we put on the throne of our hearts becomes our god, and everything else is secondary. When I put alcohol on the throne of my heart, the booze ruled my life. Instead, I let Jesus rule once more.

Perhaps it's time to ask yourself, "what sits on the throne of my heart?"

1. Ask yourself the question I posed, "If I were to lose this one thing, then my life would be over or have no meaning." Is it a romantic relationship? Your looks? A friendship? A career? Name it.

2. Why does that one item or idea have so much control over your life? What do you feel God asking you to do to put him on the throne of your heart once more (or maybe for the first time)?

I say this because some ungodly people have wormed their way into your churches, saying that God's marvelous grace allows us to live immoral lives. The condemnation of such people was recorded long ago, for they have denied our only Master and LORD, Jesus Christ.
—JUDE 1:4

There was a time in life when I was a lot harder on myself than I am now. I would freak out over the smallest mistake. Then I'd belittle myself and—in my head—remind myself what a "fuck up" I was. Yes, those are the exact words I used in my head.

Some of my self-esteem issues stem from my stepfather's expectations regarding cleanliness and chores. If I didn't perform to his standards, I'd hear about it from him. Don't get me wrong, he was a good man, just meticulous. He was a blue-collar worker whose own past caused him to take out some of his frustrations on me. So when he gave me a list of chores to do, he expected them to be done his way and within a certain time frame. As a rebellious teenager that must have messed with my psyche because over the years, I became a perfectionist who believed if I didn't do things perfectly, they weren't worth doing.

Once I became a Christian, however, I heard about a thing called grace. I learned about God's love, forgiveness, and that he saw Christ instead of my sins and shortcomings. Even though I fell short I was still loved, accepted, and clean in his eyes. Also known as the big theological word *justification*, this concept changed everything I'd ever known about expectations and standards. God's grace was like this big ocean and my sin was like a feather floating down trying to make a dent in the great blue sea.

Then something insidious happened. As I began to bask in this newfound grace in my life, I took advantage of God's precious gift and rejected his guiding hand. I viewed God's grace as *so great* it covered me even as I abused it. I guess that's the hard truth about grace, though. It covers our sin even when we abuse it, but it doesn't mean it's right.

When we abuse God's grace and continue to live in habitual sin even when we know it's wrong, it pushes us further away from him. God desires good things in our lives, but unhealthy and destructive habits only bring about dark and negative circumstances that damage our spirit. Our view of God becomes distorted as well. Have you (or do you know anyone who has) ever said, "I don't even know who I am anymore?" Sin can send us in a direction where we can't see clearly anymore. Suddenly we're lost, not following God and embracing a destructive lifestyle where our sin reigns instead of the living God.

The apostle Jude warned about how some in the early church found God's grace so marvelous, they ended up doing even more immoral things. We see the same thing happening in the Corinthian church when Paul admonishes them for getting drunk on communion wine and sleeping with their stepmoms (see 1 Cor. 5:1, 11:17-22). He points out their acts are so vile that even pagans don't engage in such practices. So why are they abusing grace?

Our sin halts our spiritual growth and drives us far from God. His grace is still there, but our bad choices lead us to stagnation. How many times have you felt distant from God while at the same time rationalizing your poor decisions? *I know I've done this plenty of times.*

In my life, this verse was a wake-up call. I questioned my motives and asked "how many things do I do that I know aren't okay? What can I do to ensure I tell a friend for accountability?" Pornography was one of those issues. I kept making excuses and would promise myself I'd "change." But I kept using porn and would tell myself, "well I'm thankful for God's grace."

Think of the destructive behaviors you justify in your mind. Maybe it's consuming pornography, hooking up, spending all our time on social media, or abusing substances. The wave of guilt you might feel is a gentle nudge from God showing us he has better circumstances for us on the horizon than staying stuck. It's important to remember that God's grace should lead us into healthy habits. Not ones that destroy us.

1. Take a moment to pray and see where you feel God nudging you. Where have you read something in Scripture that has convicted you? Write them down.

2. Are there things you are doing that you justify to yourself by saying, "well this isn't really that big a deal" or you even "that's outdated" (example: living/sleeping together before marriage)? What makes you believe this? What do the Scriptures have to say about it? If you don't know, I urge you to research and see what the Scriptures teach.

If any of you wants to be my follower, you must give up your own way, take up your cross, and follow me. If you try to hang on to your life, you will lose it. But if you give up your life for my sake, you will save it.

—MATTHEW 16:24-25

Before I ever joined my band, August Burns Red, I was a painter. From nine to five every day I would paint apartments. Then I would come home, crack a few beers, relax, hang out with friends, and then do the same thing the very next day. Rinse and repeat. But I also had this crazy desire to be the front man of a metal band and tour the world. I wanted to leave a legacy (though I had no idea what type of legacy I wanted to leave).

For a long time I settled. I accepted what life handed me and what the world offered. I lived that way because it was comfortable. Sure, I wanted a nicer car, better pay, and a romantic relationship. Who doesn't? But like most Americans, I valued comfort and the familiar in my day-to-day life. Most of us have running water, food in the fridge, internet, television, and a bed to come home to. *Why risk this comfort for a silly dream? Why rock the boat?* we subconsciously think.

Eventually, that desire to be a front man cost me my comfort. I quit my job in South Carolina and drove twelve hours to try out for August Burns Red. Then I lived with the group of guys from the band (who I had no relationship with) in an uncomfortable van for six months. I wasn't making money and specific friends and family told me that the band was using me and that I should quit and come home. It was a scary time in my life. I sacrificed my comfort and was on an unknown trajectory. But now I'm a twelve-year veteran in the metal industry.

When Jesus tells his followers to "take up their cross and follow me," he intends his statement to be shocking. The cross was a symbol of oppression and torture in the first century, and we must remember Jesus said this before he even went to the cross. His point is that, you can play it safe and keep your *comfortable* life, or you can follow Jesus. It will cost you everything and lead to intense discomfort, but you'll find *eternal* life in the process.

Far too often we can get wrapped up in our comfort. Social media, video games, going out with friends, shopping, and new trinkets numb us to the reality of our lives. It's easy to forget about God when you're comfortable, but the dreams and desires he's placed in your heart don't go away. The more you reject his calling, the more you can fall into despair because you're not willing to sacrifice your comfort to follow him. You can even end up mad at God for not fulfilling the desires he's laid in your heart because you're unwilling to step out of your comfort zone and climb the mountain.

Years ago I sat outside the Chicago House of Blues asking God what he wanted me to do to give back to my fans. His answer was HeartSupport, the very non-profit that produced this book and has helped free thousands of men and women from suicide, addiction, and abuse so they could create a legacy of life-transformation.

But to do that, once more I had to take up my cross and follow him through thick and thin. I had no idea how to start a non-profit, but I knew it was where God was leading me. With that choice came discomfort, but it has been worth it. It not only has led me to a deeper and fuller life but it also has helped thousands of others get to that same point.

Each day, Jesus is asking us to kill our comfort and pick up our cross. That cross, to every believer, is the sacrificing our fleshly desires in order to follow Christ's leading. Where's he asking you to get uncomfortable?

1. List a few desires that God has placed in your heart. What keeps you from fulfilling them? Why don't you want to?

2. Envision doing the things you've listed. What would it be like? What would it feel like? What would it do for other people? What could it do for the world, spreading God's love to others? Is it worth it?

No, dear brothers and sisters, I have not achieved it, but I focus on this one thing: Forgetting the past and looking forward to what lies ahead, I press on to reach the end of the race and receive the heavenly prize for which God, through Christ Jesus, is calling us.
—PHILIPPIANS 3:13-14

I grew up in a broken home. What I remember was a lot of verbal abuse and family division, culminating in divorce. My house was full of anger and resentment. I didn't have a father figure around until my mom got remarried, but even then my stepdad and I didn't get along.

I lived in low income housing, and for a period of time, was on food stamps. I also received reduced lunch at school. At such a young age I had a lot of burdens. Kids at school bullied me and I was still reeling from my parent's divorce. I disliked my stepdad and was trying to figure out what being a man looked like. Most days I felt like an outcast.

Like many other young boys, I lashed out in anger trying to earn respect and approval. I made careless decisions and hooked up with a lot of random girls thinking that would make me feel loved. I only felt more shame though.

I never realized just how negatively my early years impacted me until I went through a twelve-step program. (Most people assume you go through the steps because you're an alcoholic or drug addict. However, I discovered a lot of churches using the twelve steps as a recovery process for healing from all sorts of past wounds.) At first, I wasn't even sure why I was there, but I knew something was wrong with me as my past continued to haunt me.

Throughout the process, my core wounds bubbled to the surface, and I discovered I harbored a lot of resentment. My past self was—in effect—breathing toxicity into my present life. Working the twelve steps caused me to make amends and forgive those who wounded me in the past. It freed me not only to love my enemies but also myself.

In Philippians 3, the Apostle Paul reminded the church at Philippi that he still made mistakes, and his resume has mine beat. He tortured, imprisoned, and murdered Christians before his conversion, but he didn't let his past dictate his future. He pushed forward with Christ as his goal. Just imagine how much shame and guilt he could have had around that portion of his life? Instead, he didn't let his past wounds and sins dictate who he was in the present.

When I went through the steps, I realized this had to be true for me as well. I could give authority to my past to dictate who I was or how my life would play out, or I could press forward with Christ in mind and what he says about me.

When we *choose* freedom from our past, it's because we see ourselves as Christ sees us: holy and blameless due to his life, death, and resurrection that covers our past. We're not fatherless. We're not alcoholics or addicts. We're not even victims. All those words people and society have lobbed at us no longer hold any power over us because Jesus gives us a new heart and a new mind that breathes his eternal love into our being. But it's a choice, and that's the hard part. We can hand over our identity to Christ and let him impart a new one, or we can continue to believe the lies the accuser whispers to us.

As Paul reminds us, we will stumble along the way. The life of faith and our identity in Christ is a marathon, not a sprint. The goal of a marathon for most people is just to complete the race. As long as you keep running, you'll reach the finish line Don't forget to keep your eyes fixed on the finish line and on Christ, the redeemer.

1. Write one to three lies you believe about yourself that you know God would never say about you (for example: "I'm dumb" / "I'll never amount to much" / "Everyone hates me" / "I'm an addict and always will be").

2. Now take time to pray and ask God what he says about you. Write down what you hear God says about you.

3. Finally, look at your lies versus God's truth and say "I'm not a(n) _____ (idiot, addict, pervert), but God says I'm _____ (whatever God said about you).

The Spirit of the Sovereign Lord is upon me, for the LORD is upon me, for the LORD has anointed me to bring good news to the poor. He has sent me to comfort the brokenhearted and to proclaim that captives will be released and prisoners will be freed. He has sent me to tell those who mourn that the time of the LORD's favor has come, and with it, the day of God's anger against their enemies. To all who mourn in Israel, he will give a crown of beauty for ashes, a joyous blessing instead of mourning, festive praise instead of despair. In their righteousness, they will be like great oaks that the LORD has planted for his own glory.

—ISAIAH 61:1-3

These verses in Isaiah were spoken over me by a fan one evening after a show. He told me, "I believe this Scripture is what you're doing with your life and music."

I was skeptical at first, but now I believe this to be true. This Scripture is well known for being a prophetic text pointing to the Messiah. Jesus even quoted it in the synagogue in his hometown after being tempted in the wilderness (see Luke

4:18). When Jesus sent out seventy-two of his disciples, he had them fulfill this text as they brought good news and healed the brokenhearted and oppressed.

God gives each one of us different talents and abilities. I was given the ability to use my vocal chords to scream on stage, which led to a platform so I could impact people. No matter your ability, the real question is "What will you do with what you've been given?"

When we let the Spirit do his work in us, we follow in the footsteps of Christ. When you allow the Holy Spirit to work in you, Christ will lead you in his *way*. What many people don't know is that the term *Christian* never appeared until its use in Antioch (recorded in Acts 11:26). Originally, the followers of Jesus referred to their faith and the Spirit's leading as just "the Way."

Everyone on earth has this special life story to walk through or gifts to utilize as they journey on the Way. The world will try to tell you differently. The world and the devil will prey on your insecurities, struggles, pain, guilt, and shame and tell you your failures disqualify you to believe and succeed in the journey. But God's gentle voice reminds you his Spirit is upon you. You'll do great works to bring about his glory as he prompts you. But you must be sensitive enough to listen to that voice. His still, small voice clears your mind and retrains you so you can live out the life God has planned.

While you may never be a famous actor, paint a masterpiece, or be an amazing athlete, as you follow the Way, God's spirit is on you and will lead you to do amazing things. Don't buy into the social media lie that tells you you're only successful if you have thousands of followers or "likes" next to every post.

Since God formed your story, I can guarantee his Spirit will lead you to do amazing things that, though they may go unnoticed, have significant worth on earth and in the life to come—*especially for those around you.*

1. Where in your life do you believe you're underqualified or that God couldn't use you? If so, why?

2. How can you help others that are struggling (even if you are struggling)? What are some ways you can bless others today?

All Scripture is inspired by God and is useful to teach us what is true and to make us realize what is wrong in our lives. It corrects us when we are wrong and teaches us to do what is right.
—2 TIMOTHY 3:16

There was a time in my life where theology (the study of God) turned me into a religious prick. Instead of becoming more loving, gracious, and compassionate like Jesus, I became judgmental and condemned people on both the liberal and conservative sides of Christianity for their sin and "mistakes." Never mind the fact that I had numerous shortcomings (of which you've read about). I'd become so obsessed with the idea of God and his commandments that I wasn't listening to him when he spoke through the Scriptures.

In the past when I would read the Bible and pray, I'd learn something about myself and where God was leading me. But over time, my obsession with theology turned the God-breathed, life-giving Scriptures into pieces of a puzzle that needed solving. Scripture became this immovable stone that could only mean one thing or be interpreted a certain way.

One morning I woke up and headed downstairs to make coffee. While my coffee brewed, I grabbed my journal and Bible and then wrote a letter to God. I listed out how sorry I was, the sins I'd committed, and how I'd "do better" and "be stronger." I felt like I was trying to *earn* my way into God's good graces and felt the need to look up what some great theologian had to say about that. I ran upstairs to the bedroom where my wife was sleeping and cracked open my systematic theology book and began studying, writing, and taking notes word for word. When my wife woke, she found me pouring over my notes and the book and said something that became a wake-up call: "Jake, all you do is study theology. It's changing you."

She was the only person who truly saw what was happening. I was no longer moved by God's Word to grow closer to him and deepen my relationship. I was using the Bible as a checklist to make sure I had all the answers, and when I failed it meant I needed to try harder to fit the pieces of the puzzle together. I'd left grace and mercy behind and realized the Word of God was no longer teaching me because I didn't want to listen. I have since come to realize that the Scriptures are timeless. You can read one passage now, and it will speak into your current situation. But five years from now, that same passage may speak into an entirely different situation.

While reading the Bible and studying more about God is a good thing, even good things can become bad things. Food is certainly not evil. We need it to live, but it can become an obsession or a god to us. The same is true of sex. Sex is a beautiful gift from God, but if you distort it, it becomes destructive. What I had to discover was that the Bible didn't get on a cross and die for me. *Jesus did.* And through the Scriptures, the living, breathing Jesus still speaks and the words in the Bible continue to convict and draw us deeper towards him. We cannot forget that the overarching story in all the Bible is one of redemption and forgiveness. Mankind continually fails, and God repeatedly saves. Often we are the most selfish people ever when we read the Bible. We look at the circumstances in our lives and think, "I currently have this problem in my life so what verse will make me better?" Instead we should let the Scriptures read *us* and have God meet us in our mess, especially in the parts we try to hide. What we think is the problem we need fixed might not be the problem God wants to work on at that moment. We should let the Bible and God speak to our secret heart and convict us to change.

The minute we think we know all things in Scripture is the moment we know nothing. We use them as some self-help tool as opposed to letting the verses breathe life into us.

So the next time you pick up your Bible, ask God to be the one to meet you with his words not just the passage you want to cherry pick to feel better.

1. Write down a few Bible verses that catch your attention or have spoken to you in the past.

2. Ask God to speak to you about those verses and what he wants to teach you. Don't default to things like work, pleasure, or business, but areas of your heart where there's deep issues of anger, hurt, self-worth, identity, or happiness even. See what the still, small voice says and write your feelings, thoughts, and convictions. Then pray that you may be directed to take proactive steps to where God's leading you.

But to you who are willing to listen, I say, love your enemies! Do good to those who hate you. Bless those who curse you. Pray for those who hurt you.

—LUKE 6:27-28

My girlfriend cheated on me while I was on tour.

While in my early twenties when August Burns Red was just picking up steam, I'd been dating the same girl for almost two years. I was certain she would be my wife. While most of us have been cheated on, here's where the knife dug deep: she cheated on me with my best friend. The worst part was that I was still on the road with the band when I found out. I was devastated. I couldn't believe that the woman I planned to marry and my best friend had betrayed me. With my head in my hands and tears in my eyes I asked God, "Now what!? What do I do?"

Most of us are willing to forgive friends and family members for small slights they may have done. Perhaps even large ones. But I think for most of us there are people who if we were asked to forgive them, we'd think to ourselves *no way in hell.* As enlightened as we pretend to be, we have a hard time shaking the old code of "an eye for an eye" and are happy when people "get what they deserve." We even say things like "karma will get them in the end." It begs the question, however. *Have you ever felt loved or become a better person by hurting someone else or holding a grudge?* If something is broken and yet you hit it with a hammer, do you think that will help fix it?

What's interesting about these verses is that Jesus ends up taking a dose of his own medicine. First, he was beaten and flogged, then crucified with spikes driven through his hands and feet, and finally stabbed in the gut to bleed out in front of his own people. Yet, in that act of brutality Jesus took our sin upon him so we might have forgiveness. He even doubles down and forgives the people crucifying him! So when Christ commands us to love our enemies, that command isn't coming from the lips of a hypocrite. Because Christ tells us to emulate him and chose love over vengeance, he expects us to do the same no matter how horrible the situation. This doesn't mean we have to trust those who've wounded us, because trust is earned. But holding a record of wrong when Christ himself carries no record of wrong against us? That's what he expects.

Jesus is asking us to step outside our conditional boundaries of love and into a spiritual place of unconditional love. When we submit our lives to prayer for the people who have shamed us or deeply wounded us, we find freedom. We chose love over resentment, compassion over pride, and healing over pain. It's easy to make a list of reasons why someone doesn't deserve our forgiveness but looming over us is the cross, which reminds us to forgive and love those who don't deserve forgiveness.

Once we see how beautiful and loving Christ is because of his sacrifice, it helps encourage us to reflect that same grace and mercy to those who have offended us.

The day I found out about my girlfriend and best friend's betrayal, God spoke to me when I cried out. Do you want to know what he told me?

"Forgive."

I knew I needed to forgive them and move forward. So while on tour, I called both my girlfriend and my former best friend. If I'm making this sound easy, it wasn't. I had to muster every bit of strength I had because I didn't want to forgive him. I wanted to beat the shit out of him. But God's voice kept prompting me towards forgiveness, and when I talked to them and forgave them, God taught me something. By forgiving them, I didn't have to carry what they'd done in my heart. I didn't carry the burden of that wound, and it also taught me good boundaries. I learned what to accept and not accept in relationships and how to treat others like I wanted to be treated. Would you believe me if I told you I'm still friends with them? The funny part is that I am friends with both. Not as close, but my old best friend and I talk at least once a month to catch up and pray for one another.

What Jesus is trying to show us is how forgiving your enemies can move mountains in your life and bring you freedom and healing. Bitterness and unforgiveness just poisons your soul until it rots. But forgiveness breaths love. And love fuels wisdom and peace.

1. Who do you know that you need to forgive but are having a hard time doing so? Why? What did they do?

2. What steps can you take to forgive your "enemy?" Perhaps begin by just saying the words until one day you mean them. Continue to look at how Christ forgives your wrongs and let his example humble you.

*And a ruler asked him, "Good Teacher, what must I do to inherit
eternal life?" "Why do you call me good? Jesus asked him. No
one is truly good. But to answer your question, you know the
commandments: 'Do not commit adultery. You must not murder.
You must not steal. You must not testify falsely. Honor your father
and mother.'" The man replied, "I've obeyed all these commandments
since I was young." When Jesus heard his answer, he said, "There
is one thing you haven't done. Sell all your possessions and give the
money to the poor, and you will have treasure in heaven. Then
come, follow me." But when the man heard this he became very
sad, for he was very rich. When Jesus saw this, he said, "How hard
it is for the rich to enter the Kingdom of God!*
—LUKE 18:18-24

Early in my life I was obsessed with my car and video games.
Whenever I got home from work, school, or touring during my
early years in August Burns Red, there were two things I cared
about: washing or modifying my car and playing video games.
At the time, I had a Volkswagen GTi Turbo and probably

dropped $10,000 on that car alone. I added new wheels, a front mount intercooler, cold air intake, new exhaust, a shark fin antenna, and even a cup kit for suspension. Maybe that sounds like shop talk to you, but all these things took time and money, which I dumped into the car. My Volkswagen became the thing in my life that mattered most and was hard to let go of. Second to my car was playing video games like Call of Duty or EA's NHL series on my Xbox and PlayStation. Sometimes I got so sucked in I played for a solid eight hours straight!

Both "hobbies" became the distractions in my life that took up my time and what I obsessed over. I grew angry when I didn't win playing video games, and I socialized less. When I did go out, I spent time with unhealthy friends doing unsafe things. I would jump on the highway and race other cars doing upwards of 140 m.p.h. Increasingly, my car and my video games became the things that consumed me and made me happy. Were I to lose them I would have been crushed.

In life, there are simple things we enjoy that we assume aren't a big issue for us. Maybe it's a boyfriend or girlfriend. Perhaps it's cars and video games like me. A job even. Or maybe it's a good thing like your savings account. The question Jesus asks the rich young ruler penetrates our heart because we have similar idols. When I was younger, Jesus' question to me would have been "Will you sell your car and Xbox to come and follow me?" I would have flipped. Now, it might be something like "Would you quit your band and serve the homeless?" While my band is a good thing and allows me to eat and minister to people, the minute we place anything (people, possessions, careers) first in our lives is when Christ becomes secondary.

If we're honest, almost all of us have something we put over our relationship with God. In effect, what we put our time, energy, and effort into the most is what we worship. For the rich young ruler, he couldn't part with his money. For me, I couldn't part with my car and video games. It's not bad to have earthly materials as they're good gifts from God, but when we are unwilling to follow Christ when he asks for them, well, then we know what truly matters most.

Like the rich young ruler, we can talk the talk and even walk the walk. We can tithe, go to church, read our Bibles, and even serve in the community. But deep down we know when we're playing a game with God, and he'll always go straight to the heart and see what's holding us back.

Jesus will always want what you hold closest to your heart. *You know why?* Because He wants your utmost affection, adoration, and worship. Why would he even ask us to give up good things, you may ask? Every time we hand over something we hold on to tightly, it gives us the freedom to hold fast to our Savior. Each time we hand over control to Christ, he fulfills his promise for a more robust life in him.

Plus, it feels good not to be greedy. It feels great not to be addicted. It feels good not to cheat. And it feels great to live with honor and integrity in a world where often there is none.

God doesn't want just lip service from me where I look like another religious young ruler. And I'm certain he doesn't want that for you either.

1. Write three items you hold dear and would have trouble letting go of (for example, a relationship, friendship, car, job, money, self-harm, drugs, alcohol). Why don't you want to let go of those items?

2. What are three ways you can hand those items over to God and live openhanded? What do you need to do to detach yourself from them?

As Jesus approached Jericho, a blind beggar was sitting beside the road. When he heard the noise of a crowd going past, he asked what was happening. They told him that Jesus the Nazarene was going by. So he began shouting, "Jesus, Son of David, have mercy on me!" "Be quiet!" the people in front yelled at him. But he only shouted louder, "Son of David, have mercy on me!" When Jesus heard him, he stopped and ordered that the man be brought to him. As the man came near, Jesus asked him, "What do you want me to do for you?" "Lord," he said, "I want to see!" And Jesus said, "All right, receive your sight! Your faith has healed you." Instantly the man could see, and he followed Jesus, praising God. And all who saw it praised God, too.

—LUKE 19:35-43

Like most men I've struggled with pornography. My very good friend and the Executive Director at HeartSupport, Ben Sledge, studies a lot of trends about porn and speaks on the topic as he's a former addict. The statistics he's shared are eye-opening and terrifying. One survey of Christian men showed that over 50 percent of them claimed to be addicted—not just watch—but were addicted to porn.

One evening, even though I was a Christ follower, I was watching hard-core porn. At one point I remember thinking, "Is it okay to watch this!? This is someone's daughter and this guy is treating her like trash and here I am watching." You have to wonder what it does to people psychologically when they see this stuff repeatedly. Studies show porn neurologically conditions and rewires the brain. Hell, in a 2012 survey of fifteen hundred young adult men, 56 percent said their tastes in porn had become "increasingly extreme or deviant." More often we're seeing men become sexually aggressive and all the reports and abuse cases in society and our churches show it's a major problem.

You're probably wondering what porn has to do with Luke 18 and a blind beggar, aren't you?

For a long time I put porn aside as something I should be convicted about. God would approach me about what I was feeding my mind and my response was, "Yeah, okay, sounds good," but then I'd keep watching.

In this passage of Scripture we see a blind man asking for help. Not only is he blind, but Luke writes that he was poor. When he cried out for help, the crowd rebuked him. The interesting thing is, the beggar knew he was blind and in need of help. Yet no one wanted to help him. It begs the question, *who's really blind?* The blind man or the crowd?

In our lives, each of us can become spiritually blind to God's leading. Mine was porn. Each time God approached me and said, "this is an issue," like the crowd, I silenced him. I was more in love with the idea of Jesus as Savior than him being the Savior in my life. *But the poor beggar?* At least he knew where he stood and would let nothing stop him from being healed. Here was a man who had no home, no job, no money, and probably no one to care for him. He knew what he needed. Once the blind man placed his faith and everything he had in Christ, what happened? He was healed.

As a society we normalize or even laugh at numerous character flaws or shortcomings. For many men that can be porn. For others it may be an unhealthy relationship with work or someone they're dating. For some it can be issues like self-mutilation or an eating disorder. When Jesus steps in to heal us, like the crowd, we silence him. We know it's an issue but we tell ourselves "we'll deal with it later" because it's become a habit and we're comfortable for the time being or we might even think, "why bother?"

Until we've reached the end of our rope and realized how poor and blind we each are, then nothing will change. Once we're willing to cry out and let Christ heal us, that's when he steps in, but until then we're no different from the crowd, shushing the cries of our hearts and others around us.

Perhaps what we all need to realize is what author Brennan Manning once said: "A ragamuffin knows he's only a beggar at the door of God's mercy." And once we realize that, the healing can begin.

1. What is a sin you've been protective and defensive about in your life with God? Maybe you've even rationalized a destructive behavior or told yourself "it's not that big a deal."

2. If you feel God pushing on that area, why are you resistant? What is your greatest fear in admitting the truth or finding healing?

3. Now admit these areas to God and ask the Holy Spirit for some next steps. What did he tell you?

Keep on asking, and you will receive what you ask for. Keep on seeking, and you will find. Keep on knocking, and the door will be opened to you. For everyone who seeks, finds. And to everyone who knocks, the door will be opened.

—MATTHEW 7:7

When I first joined August Burns Red, we toured like madmen with little to no time off. The conditions were brutal. We would play a show and get out of the club around midnight. Sometimes we would then have to drive eight or more hours to the next venue. We lived in a van and slept on benches in the back. Two of us would drive (one to keep the driver awake), while the others slept. After two hundred miles we'd gas up and switch so the driver and passenger could sleep. We'd stop at Wal-Mart or a truck stop and shower in a sink. We usually got to the venue around two in the afternoon only to have to unload, conduct sound check, and repeat the process all over again.

When you're starting out in a band—and even when the band starts growing—you're broke. I lived at Brent's parents' house (one of our guitarists) because after each tour we'd only make five hundred to a thousand dollars each to pay bills. Eventually, the wear and tear caught up with me. After a European tour with Bring Me the Horizon, we flew back home to support Underoath for a tour. I told my manager, "Listen, I know we're trying to make the climb in our career, but I can't keep doing this. My body is wearing down." He agreed and helped get us some time off.

Putting in the work was hard, and we still toured a lot. Before the band grew, we even had conversations about what it would be like to be on the cover of *Alternative Press (AP)* magazine. AP was the magazine for the scene while I was growing up, and I'd been a fan since I was sixteen years old. Getting on the cover would have been one of my biggest dreams come true!

"Hey Brent? You ever think we'll play big festivals or tour Europe? Maybe even be on the cover of AP?"

"Yeah man, I think we will," was always Brent's reply.

If you know anything about me or my band, then you've probably found this part amusing because we've now toured Europe, Australia, Japan, and Southeast Asia. We've also landed on the cover *AP* for a special Warped Tour edition. But never in a million years would I have believed what God had in store for me next.

One morning I woke up to a text from my manager. The text read, "Congratulations boys, you've just been nominated for a Grammy!" Half asleep, I thought he was kidding and replied, "Like a *real* Grammy?" The moment I found out it was true was surreal. No one—and I repeat no one—joins a metal band thinking "Yeah dude, let's go get us a Grammy."

The average person could say, "*you* worked hard, well done!" But it wasn't me. When I first started with the band, I was a brand-new Christian, just learning how to follow Jesus. Jesus and the band were my priorities. Just like Paul wrote, "No eye has seen, no ear has heard, and no mind has imagined what God has prepared for those who love Him" (1 Corinthians 2:9), I had no idea what God had in store for me the more I followed him. But I kept on knocking and seeking, praying and asking.

I share these accomplishments not to brag, but because I thought *none of them* would be part of my musical career. As Christians, our relationship with Christ requires trust, intimacy, and action. I can pray to become a musician, but if I never take steps towards writing music and lay in bed waiting for my lucky break, is that the prayer God honors? The relationship we have with Christ requires willing participants. I love the saying "it takes two." It takes me and God to accomplish anything. I honor and love God because he loves and honors me first. He delights in honoring and bestowing good gifts on his children. Christ also puts conviction in my heart, and because I love and honor him, I act on the conviction I feel. The beautiful part about a relationship with Christ is his covenant of grace. Even when I don't honor or love God or when I neglect the conviction in my heart, He *still* loves me. Because it's a covenant and gift, nothing I do can break that bond. I can't take away what Jesus did on the cross. Salvation is a gift, and he'll never take it back.

So keep asking. Keep seeking. Knock and ask for the door to

be opened, but don't be apathetic in the process. Partner with Jesus. You just might be surprised at what happens in your life when you follow him and turn over your will and way. Doors beyond your wildest imagination can be opened. Wherever God leads you, I can guarantee it will blow your mind.

1. List two to three obstacles in your life. Then sit in prayer and ask God for a vision or word to overcome the obstacles and mountains you're facing. One by one, go down your list and write what God tells you.

2. Look back on the list weekly or monthly to focus on the future and how you can partner with God. Focus on what paths, decisions, or choices you can make to move forward in healing or overcoming your mountain.

After Jesus left the girl's home, two blind men followed along behind him, shouting, "Son of David, have mercy on us!" They went right into the house where he was staying, and Jesus asked them, "Do you believe I can make you see?" Yes, Lord," they told him, "we do." Then he touched their eyes and said, "Because of your faith, it will happen. Then their eyes were opened, and they could see!"
—MATTHEW 9:27-30

Many people have asked when I knew I wanted to be a front man for a band. My answer? *Always.* I've always known.

When I was sixteen, I started singing in a pop punk band called Smash Adams out of Columbia, South Carolina. After that fell through, I started close to five other bands. I was committed, even though each band continued to fall apart. I worked two full-time jobs—one at Hot Topic and the other at CiCi's Pizza—just to get my bands going. When I wasn't working, I'd be down in a practice shed rehearsing. I even sold my 1991 Nissan Maxima for an old Bell South cargo van so we could tour. Later, I worked for a T-shirt company and instead of a paycheck, I'd have them print off my bands shirts. When my band She Walks in Beauty broke up, it was discouraging, but I remained undeterred. While at a party one evening, a group of friends asked what I planned to do with my life. "I'm going to be a touring musician" I told them. They laughed in my face and walked off saying, "good luck with that."

Nine months later I got a text message from a friend who told me a band called August Burns Red was having vocal tryouts. The only catch was the band was in Pennsylvania and I lived in South Carolina. I let him know there was no way it would happen, but he encouraged me to shoot them an email. I got on Myspace (an old social media platform predating Facebook) and sent them some of my songs from my old band. Three days later, Brent Rambler (the guitarist) called and asked me if I would try out in person. I was painting houses at the time, but I knew I had to quit my job and try out. I informed my boss who understood and let me know I had a job if it didn't work out.

The day I drove up I was nervous. Once I arrived we went straight into the studio to record my vocals over their song "Your Little Suburbia is in Ruins." I'm sure I sucked because I was so afraid but somehow they picked me to tour with them for the next couple of months. That turned out to be a real test of faith because after each tour they weren't sure if they wanted to keep me. After one tour JB (a guitarist) grew fond of me, but Matt (our drummer) didn't want to commit to keeping me. Then on the next tour the feelings would flip and JB wasn't sold on me while Matt was!

During that time in limbo, friends and family encouraged me to quit and come home. But deep down I had faith that things would work out if I stayed the course, if I fought to be there and didn't walk away. My break came when the band toured with Between the Buried and Me and their lead singer, Tommy Rogers, had a conversation with the band, letting them know they should keep me, (Tommy, if you ever read this, thank you!)

I tell that story, because just like the blind men in Matthew 9, I couldn't see where I was going, but I had the faith to follow it through. I kept following what God laid in my heart at a young age, even when there was little hope left. It's interesting that we have two blind men who can't see where they're going, yet they follow Jesus into a house and believe he can heal them. The New Living Translation says they "followed along behind him, shouting" and then walked "right into the house where he was staying." Nothing got in their path. But more fascinating is Jesus' response to them. He tells them, "Because of *your faith*, it will happen."

In each of our lives we'll face trying times and mountains to climb. Many times we won't even know where we're going. Just like the blind men, it can feel like we're wandering around in the dark. The difference between us and the blind men is that many of us can give up whereas nothing deterred the two men seeking healing.

During tough times it's difficult to have that kind of faith and belief. Our hearts and emotions go through obstacles—just like the blind men—in order to find healing. Many times, we won't find the healing or answers immediately. The men in the story had to keep chasing Jesus and track him down. Situations will grow out of our control, failure will happen along the way, or maybe God will be silent for a while. Again, notice Jesus didn't initially respond to the men's cries for help! Yet it was their belief that carried them into the house of healing. Like the men, once we arrive at that house Jesus will ask us "Do you believe I can do it?" How we respond determines everything.

I like to remember this bit of encouraging Scripture when I'm tempted to give up. It reminds me that in difficult moments—past and present—when I've leaned on my faith, I've always ended up on God's doorstep and found an answer or healing.

Will you continue to climb the mountain even when you can't see the top? Perhaps Christ is asking you to follow him to the doorstep of healing for an answer even when he seems not to acknowledge your cry.

Keep climbing. Your faith will carry you through.

1. Take a moment and reflect on some areas where you feel you lack faith or need to trust God more. What question, like the blind men, is he asking you?

2. What actions steps can you implement to trust God more in areas you're uncertain about?

Early the next morning he was back again at the Temple. A crowd soon gathered, and he sat down and taught them. As he was speaking, the teachers of religious law and the Pharisees brought a woman who had been caught in the act of adultery. They put her in front of the crowd. "Teacher," they said to Jesus, "this woman was caught in the act of adultery. The law of Moses says to stone her. What do you say?" They were trying to trap him into saying something they could use against him, but Jesus stooped down and wrote in the dust with his finger. They kept demanding an answer, so he stood up again and said, "All right, but let the one who has never sinned throw the first stone!" Then he stooped down again and wrote in the dust. When the accusers heard this, they slipped away one by one, beginning with the oldest, until only Jesus was left in the middle of the crowd with the woman. Then Jesus stood up again and said to the woman, "Where are your accusers? Didn't even one of them condemn you?" "No, Lord," she said. And Jesus said, "Neither do I. Go and sin no more."

—JOHN 8:1-11

There have been countless times I've judged others.

There's also been several times I've been loud and vocal about it, often talking negatively behind people's backs. When I first joined August Burns Red, I would blatantly talk bad about my bandmates when they weren't around. When you live in a van with the same guys for months at a time, you butt heads. I would often say we came from the "opposite sides of the tracks," and that's why problems arose. Each of us were raised differently; we lived diverse lives; and we viewed life, politics, and situations from polar opposite standpoints. Because of our proximity in the van, it was messy, and I was judgmental. Because I was young (and young in my faith), I didn't see I was the one who had most of the issues. I wasn't in a healthy place mentally or spiritually so I would degrade those around me to feel better.

It's easy to cast stones at others when you aren't looking at yourself. With this passage of Scripture, the men who caught this woman in the very act had a "holier than thou" attitude. It's easy to compare yourself to scoundrels and never look inward. Often, we rationalize our own sin and behavior, saying "Well, I'm not as bad as (fill in the blank)." Except Jesus clearly points out a dilemma when he said, "Let him who is without sin among you be the first to throw a stone at her."

Human beings have a tendency to do this all the time. We gang up on those we don't understand, those who may not look like us, talk like us, act like us, support the same "causes," or live the same lifestyle. We compare them to our not-so-moral behavior and then, whether publicly or privately, we degrade, belittle, or condemn those we think are worse than us. But as Jesus points out, we're "all guilty and sin has no degree of difference."

Before you condemn others, examine yourself and ask, "Am I not equal to this person? Do I not struggle? Have I not committed sins that if others found out I'd be ashamed?"

Once we see ourselves in light of the gospel it humbles us, and we're able to give grace towards those stumbling and struggling. Think about how many people would feel compassion as opposed to condemnation if we took a little more time before reacting to a situation? If we remembered our own sin and how God views it no differently? I think we'd have more people dropping their stones and embracing one another, seeing the struggles we each face and knowing we're no different.

Christ is calling us to put our stones down. We're all scoundrels desperately in need of grace. Let's act accordingly.

1. Write the names of one to three people you've judged, gossiped about, or slandered. Then write what you said and what your sin was by doing so.

2. Now comes the difficult part. Pray to God for the willingness to call them and make amends. Then actually do it! Explain what you did, how it was wrong and ask forgiveness. Remember, Jesus said, "So if you are offering your gift at the altar and there remember that your brother has something against you, leave your gift there before the altar and go. First be reconciled to your brother, and then come and offer your gift" (Matthew 5:23-24). So go and be reconciled to them.

Make allowance for each other's faults, and forgive anyone who offends you. Remember, the Lord forgave you, so you must forgive others. Above all, clothe yourselves with love, which binds us all together in perfect harmony. And let the peace that comes from Christ rule in your hearts. For as members of one body you are called to live in peace. And always be thankful.
—COLOSSIANS 3:13-15

As you may have read earlier, my family life growing up was rocky. Those wounds poured over into my marriage and friendships. I could go from 0 to 60 in under a minute and it seemed like I was always jumping from highs to lows.

Throughout my youth, I partied hard and slept around to escape that deep seeded anger and resentment I felt. You think emotions like these will go away over time, but like a stain on your shirt, it requires cleaning. Once I hit rock bottom in my marriage, I saw that to make healthy changes I needed to make amends with my past.

That journey, as I've shared already, led me into a biblically based twelve-step program. My sponsor ended up being a wonderful human being named Josh Jones. Josh was a former coke addict and ran underground casinos in Texas. He used to do so much cocaine his nickname was "the coke machine." The misconception about twelve-step programs is that you have to be an addict like Josh was, but Josh explained that the Bible-based twelve-step recovery process could be for any hang-up you have. Seeing how much anger and resentment controlled my life, I stepped into the recovery process with Josh.

Each week we would set up times to talk and I would have homework to do. Then we'd work through my homework and questions, sometimes taking as long as two hours per session. But for the next year and a half I worked the steps.

One aspect that's most eye-opening about the process is discovering just how much you're at fault and not as innocent as you think. When I examined my past, I saw I was just as much at fault as some people who wounded me. I saw I needed to forgive myself and repent of the destructive behavior and make amends for the wounds I inflicted on others.

I ended up reaching out to several people in my life I harmed. I asked for forgiveness from my mother for how I spoke to her and treated her. I also reached out to my father, my sister, and many other family members. I sought resolution with my bandmates and crew members one-on-one to ask their forgiveness. I even reached out to girls I had sexual relationships and one-night stands to ask their forgiveness. It didn't always go great, but in some of those cases we both walked away feeling free. I also discovered it was just as important to forgive myself the same way I forgave others in order to let everything go.

The Apostle Paul reminds us in this verse the importance of

forgiveness and making amends. When we do so, grace covers our shortcomings. Once this process happens and we're able to let go, the peace he talks about floods our hearts. By holding onto my resentment, I was blocking not only forgiveness, but the peace promised in Christ. When we shield and hold back from God, he can't freely work within those broken areas. In my case, I held onto my wrongdoings and wouldn't let God touch them. Thus, those wounds continued to poison me until I made amends. Paul also points out another thing that happens in this process of amends: we grow closer to those we've asked a pardon from and walk in love because God forgave us first.

Today, I've become closer to everyone I asked for forgiveness and mended several broken relationships; it's done wonders in both my life and theirs.

I'm wondering what it could do for you.

1. Making amends with others shows we understand our faith deeply. Christ pardoned those who crucified him and reminds us our faith should empower us to do the same for others. Who are people you need to make amends with for ways you've hurt them in your life?

2. What can you do to make amends? Maybe you could send a text or reach out over social media to set up a meeting. Maybe you could send a card or letter.

But the Holy Spirit produces this kind of fruit in our lives: love, joy, peace, patience, kindness, goodness, faithfulness, gentleness, and self-control. There is no law against these things!
—GALATIANS 5:22-23

When we record albums for my band, we have a voting process for lyrics. During the process of writing one of our albums, I wrote twenty different sets of lyrics but only submitted the twelve I thought were the strongest.

Once we voted, I discovered *none* of my lyrics made the cut. NONE! I was shocked because that never happened before. Typically at least one or two make it into an album, but this time around nothing I poured my soul and energy into made the list. I was hurt. Part of my job as a vocalist and front man is creating memorable lyrics people love. I take pride in using a microphone to speak my life, feelings, and heart to others, and yet none of my lyrics were going to be used.

The worst part about the whole situation was that I'd be screaming lyrics I didn't write. The band is democratic, however, and lyrics I disagree with never make the cut, but the outcome was still devastating. My bandmates lyrics were just stronger. Processing the situation was weighty. *What about future albums and our recording process?* I thought. *What if I never wrote another lyric that made it onto an album ever again?*

But the whole humbling process didn't stop there.

After I record vocal tracks for an entire album, each band member gets a copy and then takes a weekend to listen and make notes. Once we head back into the studio, everyone then critiques my vocals. I enter the recording booth and everyone has changes they want to hear. I spend an entire day hearing,

"I don't like that scream."

"That sounds bad."

"The chorus isn't catchy."

"That word sounds funny. Take it out and let's find another one."

"Yikes, that sounds squeaky."

"Your scream doesn't sound full."

"Let's change that whole line and come up with something better."

The process requires me to have a lot of grace and patience with my fellow bandmates. And boy, if you don't think I'm asking God to tame my mind and tongue, you're deluded. Most times I want to rip into them as they pick apart what took me hours and weeks to create.

That's why this verse in Galatians is so important in my line of work and with the people I interact with each day. It's a reminder of what we're supposed to see in a follower of Christ when we let the Holy Spirit guide us.

When we wake up each day, we have a decision to make.

We can either be led by the Spirit or be led by our desires. Often, we can become conditioned to how society tells us we should live: for ourselves. Yet, God asks us to be *like him* as opposed to his rebellious creation. Because of our relationship with Christ we have the Holy Spirit, who, Scripture teaches, is our "counselor," "friend," and "guide." When Christ lives within us, we will exhibit love, peace, joy, patience, kindness, goodness, faithfulness, gentleness and self-control. We may not always be good at exercising these traits. I know many days I fail. Self-control is my downfall, as it is for many others. We want what we want now, and our feelings and emotions remind us "we deserve this." When we head down that path, we tend to make irrational decisions or impulsive outbursts that wound others. These days when I want to lash out or have my way, God reminds me about the fruit of the Spirit. He'd rather have me stay calm, speak softly, and listen intentionally rather than prove I'm right and win an argument. When others lash out, I can still approach them with gentleness as opposed to repaying them with harsh words.

Throughout the Bible, God asks us to sit and be still. Take time to review the ways you haven't produced the fruit of the Spirit, then turn your will and way back over to the Spirit. Remember this is a process. We can take time and think through our feelings or we can react out of anger or an offense. If we'll take the time to pray and ask God to restore the fruit of the Spirit within us, he'll honor that request and calm our nerves while guiding us through the situation. When we are renewed each day and reminded of his peace and the joy and faithfulness it produces, we're less apt to get riled up when others annoy us or make us angry. Over time, this will help us lean more fervently on God's gifts of the Spirit. The more this happens, the more the change becomes clear in the way we respond to uncomfortable moments or encounters.

Each day we have a choice: produce the love and gentleness of the Spirit or be anxious like the rest of the world in a chaotic rat race.

I think I know what each of us would prefer.

1. Where are you experiencing anxiety, anger, fear, lack of self-control, jealousy, or any other character flaw? Why do you think that's there?

2. How can you lean into your relationship with Christ daily when you feel those emotions? When a difficult scenario comes up, pause and try asking God for the fruit of the Spirit instead.

Why worry about a speck in your friend's eye when you have a log in your own? How can you say to your friend, Let me help you get rid of the speck in your eye, when you can't see past the log in your own eye. Hypocrite! First get rid of the log in your own eye; then you will see well enough to deal with the speck in your friend's eye.

—MATTHEW 7:3-5

If you've made it this far in the devotional, then you've read most of the stories about times I've been judgmental or hypocritical. Perhaps, you're wondering, though, why I didn't use this Scripture to talk about those instances. It's easy to use this verse to talk about judging others, but what's harder to talk about, and what we often neglect in this passage, is looking at a much more subversive evil: *our pride.*

Each time I've run my mouth or determined how someone else should live—without reflecting on my own issues—I fall headlong into pride. I put my own perceived "goodness" above others when I have my own log to deal with. When you're unwilling to admit your sin is just as ugly, well, Christ calls you (and me) a hypocrite.

You may have heard the expression "Stay in your lane." It means we shouldn't meddle in other people's affairs. Jesus reminds us we should focus on our own troubles rather than stirring up drama or conflict with others by judging their sin. Were we to take an honest look inward, we'd see we have our hands full. Sadly, self-reflection and humility aren't celebrated, let alone practiced, in our society. But it is something we can cultivate.

When we take time to look inward and be honest about our own struggles, the mountains we're facing, or the sin we keep falling into, that's when we find healing. When we have a healthy perspective of our own sin and standing, we can be authentic, and gentle, with others. That's when we gain the relational authority, or trust, needed to help others process their sin with gentleness.

Harping on other people's issues and belittling them is much easier than self-reflection. It's a much easier way to feel better about ourselves, but comparing ourselves to others in a haughty way is pride. That is the opposite of what God desires for us. God "opposes the proud, but gives grace to the humble" (James 4:6). The world is already a prideful place. Businesses like Wells Fargo have been nailed for greedy and self-centered practices. Celebrities reinforce our selfie culture. We take photos that share our greatest feats, but never our imperfections. Giving towards charities and churches are at all-time lows. We don't share, we don't give, we take, and yet have the audacity to say we're not selfish or prideful? When we raise ourselves above others and don't work on our own troubles, we walk away from humility and take steps toward pride. It's hard to love those around us if we're full of pride. We listen less, we care less, and we love others poorly when self-seeking affirmation rules our lives. We can't feel God's love because we feel we don't need it. After all, we're better than others, right?

The next time you find yourself quick to judge, take a moment and focus on how you've been selfish or wounded others. When you're able to recognize and admit your shortcomings, you'll discover humility. And when you discover that humility, you'll remember God loves you despite your shortcomings. And when you remember God loves you even though you are a sinner, you'll offer grace to others.

1. Take three deep breaths and clear your mind. Now ask God to reveal where there's a log in your eye or you've acted hypocritically. Write want you discover.

2. How does seeing your own "log" produce humility in you? Where can you offer grace to others this week?

For the Spirit God gave us does not make us timid, but gives us power, love and self-discipline.
—2 TIMOTHY 1:7

One afternoon I shared with my friend Ian about my threshold while playing hockey. A threshold is a line I'm comfortable getting close to, but not passing. When I play hockey, I ease up when I reach the puck and when an opponent has the puck, rather than checking him, I try to use my stick to grab the puck. I love hockey, but because I lack confidence in my ability to skate, I won't go hard or fast, and I don't try to get physical with my opponent during the battle for the puck.

Numerous thoughts run through my head regarding why I can't break past the threshold: *I could get hurt. I'm the smaller guy on the ice. What if I fall down and embarrass myself?* Each thought holds me back from becoming better and playing with passion. I want to be a better player, but I can't seem to break out of my mental rut.

My buddy Jason is like me. He loves to skateboard but

refuses to skate in front of anyone other than his friends. Any time he skates around strangers he gets anxious and nervous wondering what people are thinking of him. *Are they judging my skill and technique?* he wonders. When he dwells on these thoughts, he ends up skating worse. The threshold he can't seem to cross is learning how to skate in public and enjoy the freedom to skate anywhere.

In each of our lives, our thoughts control our dreams, action, abilities, and whether we love others well. The fear that creeps in so easily can hold us back from becoming the person God has destined us to be. Timothy reminds us that in Christ we don't have a spirit of fear or timidity. In Christ, each of us has the power to overcome our fears because there's no reason to be afraid when you have the creator of the universe on your side. We each have the power to wrestle control back from fear and anxiety. That begins with countering the lies we tell ourselves and bold actions that make us strong and courageous.

As of the time of this writing, I have a hockey game to play this evening. Tonight, I will entrust my thoughts and fear into God's loving care, and maybe then I'll finally burst through the threshold.

I hope you do too.

1. What fears and anxieties play on repeat in your mind? Write them down.

2. Now that you see them on paper, write how they're keeping you from the life you want and future goals.

3. Each time your fears and anxieties pop up, do this exercise: Quote 2 Timothy 1:7: *"For God has not given us a spirit of timidity, but of power, love, and self-discipline."* Then ask God for his thoughts and peace to wash over you so you may take a bold action step!

For we who worship by the Spirit of God are the ones who are truly circumcised. We rely on what Christ Jesus has done for us. We put no confidence in human effort."
—PHILIPPIANS 3:3

Growing up without a father figure was difficult. My biological father was around for weekends and holidays, but after my parent's divorce it wasn't the same. Without his influence, it became a challenge to be a young man in the world without guidance. So I looked up to older men to be father figures in my life because I had no clue what a father, husband, or even just being a man meant. The lack of love from a father also caused me to look for unconditional love from friends. Eventually, I tried working my ass off to show the world I was worthy of love and respect. My life became about performance just so I could get a pat on the back. Throughout much of my life I've been a chameleon, changing my mask to fit other people's expectations and standards of who I'm supposed to be.

As my relationship with Christ grew, I was fathered by God

and discovered true love and acceptance. God's unconditional love has now become the most comforting and reassuring treasure in my life. In order for God to love me, I don't have to talk, act, or look a certain way. I'm not required to join a club, pay dues, or even wear the right clothes or have money in my bank account. I don't even have to go to church in order for God to love me!

Don't believe the lie that in order for God to love and accept us, we have to be good. God doesn't want my good behavior or clean-cut lifestyle. *He wants just me.* He doesn't care if I'm covered in tattoos and bald with a giant beard. He loves me despite my shortcomings and sins. God simply loves me for who I am—*his son.*

Christ is the only person who exists that loves me fully and completely. He knows me on the deepest and most intimate level. He knows my most pure thoughts and my most disgusting and depraved ones. And yet, he loves me.

The Apostle Paul reminds us that because of what Christ has done for you and me, we don't have to run around and earn God's love. It's not about our effort; it's about Christ's sacrifice on the cross—and that he died while we still despised him. We can't earn his love. It's freely given.

All those years I spent searching for approval and love, I was really looking for Jesus. And perhaps you are too. Perhaps you're still trying to earn God's love and "be better." Maybe you're looking to friends, a romantic relationship, or a job to tell you you're accepted. They'll always let you down though. Friendships begin and end, and some will end in betrayal. Success and popularity lose their luster and a job can only provide minimal satisfaction. They're temporal and minimal compared to the unconditional love God offers us through his son. In my life, several people have abandoned, betrayed, or used me. I've had people pretend to be my friend when they're really snakes. Their love was often conditional and the very definition of a "fair weather friend." Many times I've heard of people disowning a friend or severing a relationship because the other person didn't "act right" or didn't do what they wanted them to do. God's love, however, comes with no conditions. He has never abandoned, betrayed, or left me. When you place your life in Christ's hands and believe what he says about you, you find freedom, and he molds you. But if you trust man over God? It's disastrous. Other people can't give you the unconditional love you crave, so why not place all of it in Jesus?

These days Christ whispers in my ear which paths to take, and because I know he loves me, I trust him. I then care less about what men and women expect of me because they're not my Father, Lord, or Savior. They're just humans like me.

When you begin to accept Christ's love and stop trying to earn it, you'll forgive the unforgiveable rather than keeping a scorecard. You'll give mercy to the marginalized and not worry about how it makes you look in front of others or in God's eyes. You'll simply do it because you love God. And then you'll have no doubt he loves you too.

1. Reflect on Christ's crucifixion for a few minutes. How in his death did he show unconditional love to you and the world?

2. How are you trying to earn approval either from people or God? Why?

3. Write a list of moments in which you've felt God's love. This can be something as simple as winning a soccer match or watching a sunset.

Trust in the LORD with all your heart; do not depend on your own understanding.

—PROVERBS 3:5

One of my close friends living in South Carolina got addicted to heroin. She's extremely intelligent with a big heart, so it was odd to me that she got into using. Due to her past and some family issues she unfortunately fell into the wrong crowd.

We would often talk late into the night and sometimes she would call thinking she would die. One evening, she called shortly after I returned home to Pennsylvania from tour. She was having a full-blown panic attack and asked me to talk her down. I told her we had to act now. I let her know if she was serious about checking into rehab, even though I just got home, I would drive all the way to South Carolina and help check her in. She agreed, so I left early the next morning.

When I got to her apartment, she was drunk at the pool, hanging out with some random guys. I took her back to her apartment, got her cleaned up, and then into my car. Once we arrived at the facility, I looked at her and asked, "Are you ready?" She panicked and told me she couldn't do it. She ended up talking to the clinic but convinced herself she didn't need rehab and walked away.

That was an experience that hurt a lot. As much as I wanted to help her and love her through this process, I realized I couldn't. God was asking me to walk away, but it seemed so counterintuitive! *Weren't we to love the broken and struggling like He did?* I had to trust the Lord and lean not on my own understanding. There was no way I could change her heart. God would have to be the one to do that. I knew deep down she had to hit rock bottom and want recovery for herself. While helping her seemed right and good, it wasn't what she needed. So I walked away and let go of her.

There will be times in all our lives where Christ asks us to make decisions that seem backwards or uncomfortable. That may not even feel right. But God is asking us to step aside and let him breathe into the situation.

Once I gave up control and trusted God—even though I didn't understand how good could come of this—she hit rock bottom and got clean. I'm happy to report she's been clean for over ten years now. Through that experience in my life, I saw I needed to let God lead me in deciding how to love a friend. I realized I had to let go and have faith in God for her to find healing. I was the one getting in the way.

To have God move mountains, we have to trust the God response and not just the "good" response. When we do, we'll watch the impossible happen.

1. Consider someone in your life who needs help. Are you setting boundaries or enabling bad behavior?

2. Take time this week for prayer and self-reflection and ask God to show you where you're choosing your way over his will. Is it pleasing to you? Or are your actions pleasing to God?

Dear brothers and sisters, if another believer is overcome by some sin, you who are godly should gently and humbly help that person back onto the right path.

—GALATIANS 6:1

You know already that I went through a painful and messy divorce that led to poor decisions, depression, and alcohol abuse. What you may wonder is how I made it out of that rut to see the sun again.

After my divorce was finalized, I would sulk around in shame and despair. I believed I was a failure because my marriage failed. I would pick up the phone and call my friend Isaac. For months Isaac would listen to me weep and mourn the loss of my marriage. He would listen to the same regrets and hurt over and over, yet he continued to call me every day. He didn't just let me wallow in self-pity, though, he encouraged me to go to therapy and even prayed with me. Even when I was drunk, and it was late, he'd pick up the phone at three in the morning.

Through his unconditional love, gentleness, and humble

correction I started to heal. I began to see there was more in this life than what I "felt." The greatest lesson Isaac taught me and reminded me of was that I wasn't worthless or a failure. Because I believed I failed in marriage and wasn't seeing myself as a child of God, I ran headlong into sin. . Isaac showed me how my view of Christ was distorted and how I was forgiven and loved deeply. Isaac helped guide me out of my depression and get back on my feet. God used Isaac to show me his never-ending compassion and love during one of the most devastating seasons of my life.

In life, each of us will have seasons where we blow it and run from God. When the pressure of life is too great, sometimes we believe we won't make it past today. Our judgment becomes clouded and we can't see clearly, so we kinda just give up and run toward our sin. The next thing we know, we're on an unhealthy path, and we need a brother, sister, or a good friend to extend their hand and help us up once more. That's what Galatians 6:1 is describing.

But there's a forewarning in this verse. The helpful brother (or sister) has to be humble and gentle. Far too often when Christians blow it, we find condemnation from other believers instead of a gentle spirit. This Scripture describes a man or woman who can reach into the muck and wipe off the wayward brother. Someone who can correct our posture with gentleness. This person needs to dig deep to figure out where we went wrong, where we are headed, and how we can get back on track. It takes blood, sweat, and tears and is an investment that sometimes doesn't always work out, but that's what Scripture commands of us.

The question we must ask ourselves is how do we see a

brother or sister when they fall down? Do we see only the mud they're caked in? Or do we see the masterpiece waiting to emerge?

1. Has a friend come beside you to help you figure out or overcome a struggle, issue, or sin in your life? List a few examples where this has happened and what they did that made you feel loved, respected, and understood.

2. Is there anyone in your life right now that could use that same grace and love? What can you do to reach out and support them?

They will eat and still be hungry. They will play the prostitute and gain nothing from it, for they have deserted the LORD.
—HOSEA 4:10

When most people think of idols or false gods, they often think of drugs, alcohol, or materialism. However, idols and false gods can also be ideas or tangible items we elevate above God. The harsh reality, though, is that we often elevate every day desires above our Creator. For instance, I've put my desire to be a musician above God before. I've also put the work I do with HeartSupport above God (and HeartSupport is a ministry!). A job, relationship, social media, hobbies, or even food can become things we can elevate above God. They're not inherently evil or bad, but when we turn to them for satisfaction or to "fill our cup" they become idols.

The reason any of us chase after idols is that we believe they can make us feel full or complete. For a time, they do. Then the bitter end comes and once more we go searching. It's like taking medication that wears off, not the cure that heals us.

These false gods can never fulfill like Christ can. In the heart of every man and woman there's a deep desire to be unconditionally loved. So when we reach for things like fame, it's because we want to be recognized, and through recognition we believe we've earned love. When a loved one showers us in gifts and affection, the material items give us a temporary sense of satisfaction and we feel love from the gift giver. But it doesn't last long. The same is true of every romantic relationship. The butterflies will fade and love becomes a choice besides a feeling. When we look to these things for significance, we're always left grasping at the wind when what we desperately want is an eternal source of love.

Through Christ's sacrifice on the cross, we see the picture of unconditional love. While we were yet sinners, Christ died for you and me (see Romans 5:8). If you can wrap your head around the fact that no sane person would die for an enemy, you get a glimpse into God's crazy love.

And that's the key to this passage of scripture in Hosea. Because God's love is the only source of eternal fulfillment in life, that's what we should chase after. Everything else is like a dying man drinking sand from a well. Throughout the book of Hosea, God reminds Israel they've turned their back on him by choosing to follow other gods. Like Israel, you and I do the same. So God reminds us that when we chase after idols, we will never be full. We'll always thirst for more.

Because God planted eternity in our hearts (see Ecclesiastes 3:11), we won't ever be content with misplaced worship. Our devotion to idols and false gods leads us to an empty road. Yet, in Christ, we can know fulfillment.

Because Christ died for our wrongdoings, he bridges the gap between God and His creation (us). By bridging that gap, we experience joy, love, and fulfillment. When we turn our backs on him and chase other gods, he becomes jealous. That may sound harsh or strange but imagine it like this: Say I raised a son and loved him and showered him with gifts. Then one day when he's older some deadbeat comes along and woos him away, only to get him involved in a life of drugs. Then my son starts calling the other man his "father." Naturally, I'd be jealous and want my son back! With God, it's the same. He wants his sons and daughters back, so they can experience true life and be satisfied.

It's important to remember that people can only love to the extent of their understanding of love. If you know Christ and his love, you will feel loved and accepted. You will then offer that love to others. But when we chase after this world, we won't know God's love and will continue to be hungry and thirst for more, and have nothing to give to others.

Each day Christ reminds us we have a choice: Fulfillment in him or sand from a dried-up well.

1. Write down a few idols or false gods that come to mind. These can be good things as I've explained, but they take your time, energy, and devotion away from God.

2. What do you see happening when you turn to these idols? Is it to relieve anxiety or stress? How do you believe they help you cope or fill you up?

3. What do those false gods give you that you feel you can't receive from your relationship with God? How can you turn your will and way over to God to find fulfillment?

That is why the Holy Spirit says,
"Today when you hear his voice,
don't harden your hearts
as Israel did when they rebelled,
when they tested me in the wilderness."
—HEBREWS 3:7-8

One summer on Vans Warped Tour, I'd been discussing the lineup of the bands with some buddies while we were working outside our trailer. There was a specific band on that tour I found to be quite offensive. I really didn't like the way they portrayed themselves on stage and didn't support their message. However, I didn't explain it like that when talking to my friends. Instead, I ran my mouth and just talked mad shit about them. As I was belittling them, I felt a sensation like something stuck me in my side. Even though I felt justified in how I felt towards this band, I felt guilty for saying all the degrading, belittling things about them. I tried to push it out of my mind, but the guilt would come and go for the next week.

One day after I finished playing my set with August Burns Red, I was walking back to cool off in our tour bus and saw the bus of the band I'd been trash talking. They parked their bus just two or three spots away from us. As I walked past their bus, once again I felt that conviction. I stopped for a moment and asked God in my head, "What man? What do you want me to do? Ask for forgiveness or something?" After all, I had said nothing *in front* of them! But I felt that was what God wanted me to do.

So I went to the door of their bus and knocked. One of their crew guys opened the door and I asked if the band was on board. He nodded and invited me inside, so I stepped in, greeted everyone, and then sat down. Our conversation started with small talk. They asked how I was doing and how my show went. I told them it was great because we had a great crowd and that their crowd would be insane too. Then the moment came to explain why I was there, so I just said it. I told them I had been talking shit and judging them behind their backs, so I wanted to apologize. They were pretty surprised and called it "a pretty ballsy move." But they respected what I did and accepted my apology. We then hung out the rest of the night talking and laughing together.

I still don't agree with their message on stage and our lifestyles are very different, but I chose to respect and care about them as human beings. Once I gave them a chance, I found some things in common and discovered they were genuinely nice guys.

A lot of times as Christians, we know how to do the right things and avoid decisions that will cause other people to think bad of us. We don't, however, choose the right path because of what God would think of us. We might give our money away and volunteer. We might avoid drugs, sex, or binge drinking so people will think we're "good Christians" and pat us on the back. But God looks at the heart. He often asks us to step out in faith and act on what he's told us even in situations where we normally lack the courage to follow through. We should be attentive to what we feel God is telling us to do at the moment even though a lot of times the thing he may be asking us to do can feel uncomfortable.

The message to the church in the book of Hebrews is the same. The author reminds them of a Psalm where they're told not to harden their hearts against God's leading like they did when they wandered around in the desert for forty years with Moses. When we harden our hearts against God's leading, we enter the desert. Often when I find myself in the desert and ask, "Why did you lead me out here God?" I realize I'm the one who wandered away from his guidance and am reaping the consequences of my actions.

That's why I was glad I followed the Lord's prompting in that instance when I experienced a lot of guilt. I felt God telling me it wasn't right of me to talk about anyone unkindly. He prompted me to apologize even though they probably never would have found out. The whole scenario is something I wouldn't have done on my own, but because I didn't harden my heart, I learned more about God's compassion. We have the opportunity to have some amazing and humbling experiences if we're willing to risk obeying Him. I learned that following God isn't just about following a bunch of rules. It's about listening for God's voice and trusting Him enough to believe and do what He says. I suggest listening a little more to your spirit when you interact with people around you and see if you don't get a tug from God to go the extra step.

1. Think about a situation that doesn't sit right with you right now. Is God calling you to take a risky step with a person, your job, your church, or something else?

2. Building up your relationship with God where you can hear Him takes time because we have a tendency to be hard hearted. Reach out to people you know who love God. How do they connect with Him? Do any of those things sounds like a cool, new way to get to know God?

Walk with the wise and become wise;
associate with fools and get in trouble.
—PROVERBS 13:20

When I was growing up in Columbia, South Carolina, I wasn't cool. I hung out with the punk rock kids, and with the "yo" boys and more gangster types. Maybe because of the crowd I chose, I got bullied a lot throughout middle school and high school. I remember being called a "faggot," and before class one afternoon, a bully slammed my head on the desk and punched me repeatedly in the back of the head. I cried in front of my peers that day.

Another time I got bullied was when I dated a girl named Kionna. Her brother didn't like me because I was white. He roughed me up in the hallway once and told me to stop dating his sister. Then not long after that, I got into a fight during class because a kid wouldn't stop pushing my desk. He'd been bullying me for the entire school year. One day I got tired of it. I told him if he pushed my desk one more time, we were gonna fight. Sure enough, he pushed my desk the minute the words left my mouth. So I got out of my seat and punched him straight in the face.

In those environments, it seemed like the only way to get someone to stop screwing with you was to be verbally and physically aggressive. So to survive and cope with all of my frustration, I turned into the very thing I hated and was ruining my life: a bully.

I remember bullying one guy in particular. Kyle wasn't popular, and I said some downright mean and belittling things to him. Once as some other bullies and I were getting off the bus in middle school, we pushed him to the ground and began punching him. I think my buddies and I made him cry a few times a week. Now I feel awful for the things I said and did.

For a few years I was in and out of the principal's office for bullying. At the beginning of my senior year, my mom sent me to an alternative school called Chapin Alternative Academy. The school is where all the "bad kids" go when no one else could deal with them. What most people didn't see, however, was that those of us who ended up there were misunderstood.

Chapin started out with ten or twenty kids, but by the end of the year we had a couple hundred students. Over time, more kids showed up who'd been kicked out of their schools and came to the Academy as a last resort. Unfortunately, because of the troubled youth there, it also became a prime location for bullies. To protect myself, I made friends with the bullies and proved I was worth having around. But that also meant I had to do more bullying.

Looking back, what I've noticed is that bullies become bullies because at some point they were picked on too. Someone abused them verbally or physically, so they take out their hurt and anger on others. Many schoolmates hurt and disrespected me, and because of that pain I responded by becoming a bully to someone else, which I deeply regret.

During my time at Chapin, I met a few people that changed the course of my life. I owe a huge thank-you to Mr. Walker, Ms. Searfass, Ms. Cruea, and all my teachers during my adolescence. No one in my neighborhood or at school treated me like I was worth anything. But the teachers became some of the first people in my life that made me feel like I mattered, and that the choices I made were important. They helped get me on track and even came out to my band's shows to support me.

A turning point came when one of my teachers sat me down and pointed out the reality of what was happening to many of my classmates. They were joining gangs, dropping out of school, getting pregnant, doing drugs, and making choices that could ruin the trajectory of their lives. My teacher then asked me, "Is that really the direction you want to go?" The question caught my attention, and I ended up altering the path I was on.

In the book of Proverbs, Solomon instructs his son in the ways of the wise to keep him from making mistakes and to think about the company he keeps. Were he to sit here among us today perhaps he would ask this question of you: *Who are the voices in your life that matter, and how are they influencing you?* Think about your family, friends, teachers, people at work, church even, or school. Are they helping you to become the person you want to be? Or are they more like the voices I had in my life before Chapin, making you believe you're worthless? Do you have to do things that don't honor God just so you can belong or survive?

We need to examine whose voices we're listening to, and question their messages. But if we aren't careful choosing who influences our lives, then we're taking a huge risk. We have the potential to head in a painful and harmful direction, just because we're not seeking men and women of character and wisdom.

If you don't like your life, or the direction you're going, maybe you need to find new voices to tell you the truth about who God made you to be, and what you're meant to do in this world.

And like me, it may alter your life's path for the better.

1. Who do you listen to the most in your life (even if you don't really like them)? Who do you allow to tell you who you are, and how the world works? Are the messages they send you true? Hopeful? Respectful? Compassionate? Empowering?

2. If you need more positive voices in your life, where can you look? Is there anybody in the places where you do life (like work or school) that you should seek out?

Stay true to what is right for the sake of your own salvation and the salvation of those who hear you
—1 TIMOTHY 4:16

If you haven't figured it out yet, *I'm not perfect.*

When the team at HeartSupport approached me about writing a devotional, I was excited but hesitant. I wanted to be authentic and honest and that meant leaving in a lot of messy content that typically gets flagged within Christian circles. But I was determined to stay true to my experiences and encourage those who wanted to deepen their relationship with God or those spiritually seeking. This devotional is a testament of the miracles and mountains God has worked and moved in my life. The sole reason I poured out my heart here is because I want people to get to know God like I do.

By now, I hope you've seen the way he's changed my life and heart. Even in the moments where I thought he was distant and not listening, I can look back see God was in each instance providing strength and security. I hope that by taking off my mask and showing you my flaws, you'll take yours off as well and stop pretending for others. I've busted my tail studying to make sure you're getting solid content. Two pastors on our staff reviewed this book. I'm not sure everything is perfect in here, but God only asks each of us to try. The rest is up to him.

To those of you who've made it to the end, I pray this book has been an encouragement. It's been a joy to share how Christ's love has changed me and is changing me. I hope you see Christ as I do—a father, brother, teacher, healer, counselor, a hug, the King, and a safe haven. Whether you've been the victim of sexual assault or committed it, you're loved by our Creator. God knows no boundaries on who he'll accept into his kingdom. As I've said countless times to my fans: it doesn't matter if you struggle or not, whether you're gay or straight, black or white, racist or loving, an addict or alcoholic, from another religion or super-religious—you're all welcome and loved at HeartSupport because Christ asks me to love my neighbor as myself. That's staying true to what is right and is the testimony of my salvation.

God loves you and in the deepest parts of my heart—with this verse from Timothy as my witness—this is the truth about Jesus Christ and His love for every human being on this earth.

I hope that this book has encouraged you to see God in a deeper way and to seek more of his love. For we cannot truly love if we do not know the God who loves. Let us love with his love and choose his love daily.

"And may you have the power to understand as all God's people should, how wide, how long, how high, and how deep his love is. May you experience the love of Christ,

through it is too great to understand fully. Then you will be made complete with all the fullness of life and power that comes from God."

—EPHESIANS 3: 18-19

1. Write out your story. All the good, bad, and ugly.

2. Where did you see God intersecting? How can you use your story to encourage others and as a testament for those who may not know God?

All praise to God, the Father of our Lord Jesus Christ. God is our merciful Father and the source of all comfort. He comforts us in all our troubles so that we can comfort others. When they are troubled, we will be able to give them the same comfort God has given us.

—2 COR. 1:3-4

On the final run of Vans Warped Tour in 2018, we created a giant "Support Wall" where each day our staff wrote the personal stories of men and women who needed encouragement and support. People at Warped Tour overwhelmingly responded by sharing their heart, hopes, and personal demons.

As I saw the responses each day, I noticed something that rattled me. There were several responses in which people shared about their sexual assault or rape. For several years we gave out a book written by a personal friend of mine named Justin Holcomb. It's a book for victims of sexual assault and abuse entitled, *Rid of My ~~Dis~~Grace*, (which I highly recommend and helped me). Yet, as movements like #MeToo and #ChurchToo have grown, so has our awareness as victims come forward with their stories.

So it's time I came forward too.

I was sexually assaulted as a child, but it wouldn't be the only incident in my life. Later in life, I had a traumatic event in college where I was touched inappropriately. I won't go into details, but both events messed me up. As a kid, the assault confused me. I didn't know what to do with the experience, and I certainly didn't want to tell anyone. Assault seemed like something that didn't happen to men. Years later, I would discover I wasn't alone. Statistically, one in six men have been sexually assaulted, as have one in four women.

I carried the shame from my sexual assault for years when I was younger, and it was difficult for me to be intimate with anyone. I felt ashamed and like I "wasn't a man." Men and women can react in one of two ways to their sexual assault either avoiding all contact or acting out because of what happened. I was the latter case in which I slept around a lot, trying to prove I was man enough.

The voice in my head always told me, "tell *no one* about this." Far too often when a victim comes forward they're met with blame, disbelief, suspicious questions, shallow platitudes, bad advice, or toxic theology. We're met with comments like, "No, that didn't *really* happen," or "you deserved it because you put yourself in that situation." I can't tell you how crushing this is for those of us who've endured the abuse. No one "*deserves*" to be assaulted.

Processing everything I had to rely heavily on God's comfort once I was ready to move forward. There were times of mourning and weeping, loneliness, or trying to use sex to fill the void, but God came along to comfort me. The thing about sexual abuse is that when you don't feel you can talk to anyone about it, God already knows and wants to comfort you. Any time I wanted to process or talk about what happened, God always showed up. He was sympathetic and nurturing throughout the entire process of healing while I reflected on the wrong done to me. My wounds healed with time and today I'm able to share about my assault to comfort others and say, "*I know. It happened to me too.*"

That's what this verse in 2nd Corinthians reminds me of. That God comforted me in my darkest times so I could comfort others in theirs. Whether or not you've been a victim of sexual assault, you still have the same Holy Spirit in you that can comfort others when they're troubled or hurting. Maybe you've been an addict and can help other addicts. Maybe you've been depressed or anxious and can help others who are. Maybe you've never experienced what other people have? You can still be a source of comfort and love for them.

God taught me through my pain that I'd been hurt by hurting people. Evil will always try to use flawed people for its purposes to destroy this world. Once I discovered forgiveness, however, I became a person who began to heal, and healing people heal other people.

So today, if you feel hurt, confused, exhausted, or lonely, lean into God's great comfort. Allow him to walk in the pain with you especially if you've been a victim of sexual abuse like I have. Your future is waiting in his hands where he gently wants to restore you.

And when that happens? *You'll know how to comfort others.*

1. Where have you been wounded in the past? Is it still difficult to process or move forward? Why?

2. How can you lean into God and the comfort he promises? How can you comfort others with His love?

3. If you feel God pressing on you to reach out, perhaps an action step looks like sharing with a safe friend or family member an event that still haunts you. What would keep you from doing so? Why? How can you combat that and trust God?

Coming from a broken home to become a two-time Grammy-nominated musician, Jake Luhrs has toured over forty different countries and sold over half a million records as the front man of metal band, August Burns Red. Over eight years ago he laid the foundation for the nonprofit HeartSupport that now helps more than ninety thousand people a month. Through Jake's influence and leadership, the organization has encouraged thousands to take steps of healing in overcoming depression, self-harm, addiction, eating disorders, and several other issues while spreading the importance of mental and spiritual health among his colleagues and the music industry. In 2016, Jake was presented an Alternative Press Music Award for Philanthropy because of the impact HeartSupport made in the music industry. Jake is most passionate about his personal and intimate relationship with Christ because of the many ways in which he's seen God impact his life and others. When not on tour, he resides in Pennsylvania with his French bulldog, Winston.

HeartSupport was created by Grammy-nominated musician Jake Luhrs of metal band August Burns Red. After seeing his fans struggling through the same issues and addictions he went through growing up, he wanted to use his platform to impact a generation. In 2016, the organization won a Philanthropy Award in recognition of their work at the Alternative Press Music Awards. In 2017, the organization was recognized as one of the top 100 nonprofits in the world for social innovation. The team at HeartSupport often travels around the United States educating churches, nonprofits, and other organizations, while weaving engaging content along with statistics to inform and train their audiences regarding issues facing today's generation.

D W A R F ♀ P L A N E T

A PRACTICAL GUIDE THROUGH DEPRESSION

DEPRESSION FEELS LIKE LIVING ON A DISTANT DWARF PLANET.

THIS BOOK IS YOUR WAY OUT.

In 2006, Pluto was downgraded to dwarf planet status. Jokes were written and memes were shared. Today, Pluto isn't taken as seriously as its larger brothers and sisters in the solar system. And on a related note, depression has never been taken as seriously as its counterparts. It can safely be called the Dwarf Planet of our mental health crisis.

That ends now. The book you hold in your hands is the result of years of coaching, studying, winning, failing, and talking to hundreds of people. In these pages, you'll discover new facts about your depression and find ways to navigate the obstacles that stand in the way.

If you're in the midst of depression, simply opening *Dwarf Planet* may feel overwhelming. We urge you to overcome. Read it each day, engage with the content, and complete the exercises. By the end, you will be shocked by how much you've learned and grown.

Climb in. *We're going to get you off this rock.*

ReWrite

THE JOURNEY FROM
SELF-HARM TO HEALING

*Self-Harm, Self-Injury, Cutting—Hope for a Generation,
Help for Families*

Many in the emerging generation have found themselves in a hopeless cycle of self-harm. Whether it's cutting, burning, hair pulling, or beating themselves up with guilt and shame, they can't get out of the same rut. Most aren't even sure why they do it. All they know is that for some reason, it helps.

For men and women across the globe, it may seem like nothing will get better. Most believe no one understands self-harm or that real help is elusive and hard to find.

If that sounds like you, we have good news. You're not sick, crazy, or doomed to hurt yourself for the rest of your life. ReWrite will help clear up the stigmas and reasons behind self-harm, tackle the hard topics of guilt and shame, and provide the proven steps to bring you to a place of hope and healing. And if you're a concerned family member or friend, you'll finally understand what's going on and how you can help.

Join others who have successfully turned their lives around with information provided here.

Step into the journey. ReWrite your story.